www.xulonpress.com

In Loving Memory of
Jim Sr. and Jim Jr.

With many happy memories of
you both eating popcorn and
watching the game. Go Twins!

TABLE OF CONTENTS

The Miracle of

FORGIVENESS

66 With God all things are possible. 99
Matthew 19:26

INTRODUCTION

It's been over five years since God first placed on my heart the idea of writing a book on forgiveness. When I first sat with pen in hand (yes, I still write the old fashioned way), I did just that, I sat. Nothing flowed through my pen. I began waiting on God... and waiting... and waiting. I knew that the task was beyond me. While I have experienced the miracle of forgiveness, it is one thing to experience it, and another to put it into words.

How does one even attempt to put words to the supernatural? There is nothing natural about forgiveness — it is supernatural. God's thoughts are not our thoughts and His ways are not our ways. Finally, I put down the pen.

All of a sudden the stories came. This is simply a book of real life stories. Some of them are mine, some belong to people from long ago, and some of them are Jesus' stories retold.

Jesus often used parables, or stories, to help people understand spiritual truths.

Forgiveness is a miracle that once experienced, must be kept in the forefront of our minds and kept fresh in our hearts. We are quick to forget. Part of the miracle will be to see the truth that will lead us to forgiveness. The other part of the miracle will be to help us hold onto that truth.

That is my prayer for each of us. That God will make us able to forgive, and keep us able to forgive.

Chapter One

SAM AND BEN

I used to be a school teacher. Physical education and health. That's right; I used to be an athlete. "Martians and Mushrooms" was the game that all my kids wanted to play. Every grade, either gender. They loved it. It was nothing more than a glorified game of dodge ball. Everyone started out as a Martian. They would all run around trying to avoid the person with the ball. Whoever had the ball would throw it at a person and try to hit them. The rule was you had to hit them below the waist. Rules are very important when you're a phy-ed teacher. Without rules people get hurt. If you got hit by a ball (below the waist) you would turn into a mushroom and you'd have to sit on the ground with your legs crossed until by chance you were able to catch a fly ball. Then you were a Martian again — you'd be back in the game.

I had a fifth grade class that particularly loved the game. Ben and Sam were in that class. They were best friends. They were very different, but in spite of their differences, they were best friends. Sam was an athlete. If you were picking softball teams, Sam would be the first guy you'd pick. Ben was good at a lot of things, but sports was not one of them. If you were picking softball teams, Ben would be the last picked. That's why I never let them pick their own softball teams.

I started the game one rainy day by handing the ball to Ben, thinking that he would at least get to handle the ball once during the game. Ben rushed into the mob of kids, aimlessly threw the ball and unintentionally hit Sam. All-star Sam was out of the game — at the hands of Ben no less. Sam was not happy.

Sam sat as a mushroom for at least five, possibly even ten minutes, before he finally caught a fly ball. He was back in the game, and he was back with a vengeance. He had his sights set on one person and one person only — Ben. Sam was a man on a mission.

Sam chased Ben down until he finally cornered him. He wound up and threw the ball harder than any fifth grader should be able to throw a ball. And when he threw that ball he was not concerned about the rules.

Back when I was teaching phy-ed they didn't have the nice, soft, safe, nerf balls that exist today. No, back then all we had were red rubber balls. So when Sam hit Ben smack in the face, it hurt — a lot. Ben started to cry.

Now, in spite of a changing culture that stresses the importance of men learning how to get in touch with their emotions, that day in the gym was no time for a discussion on how it's okay for guys to cry. This was Ben;

this was the fifth grade; this was serious.

Ben slowly took himself out of the game. Head bowed low, unable to hold back his tears, he walked across the entire length of the gym to the far corner. He leaned against the wall, slid to the floor and put his head between his knees.

I called Sam over and asked, "Sam, what was that about?"

"Sorry."

"Are you really sorry?"

Sam shrugged. "Yeah."

"You might want Ben to know you're sorry."

"Yeah." And then Sam turned to run and tell Ben he was sorry — run, mind you, because this was Sam and he was anxious to get back in the game.

But I called him back, "Wait a minute Sam, come here. Do you think that when you run over there and quick tell Ben you're sorry that he is going to believe you?"

Sam paused. "Probably not."

"And then when he doesn't accept your apology will you be a little mad at him, because after all, you will have said you're sorry?"

Sam asked, "What else can I do?"

"I think Ben wants to believe that you are sorry. But

sometimes a person needs time to believe that we are really sorry. Not just time to get over it, but time to believe it."

Sam listened silently.

> *Sometimes a person needs time to believe that we are really sorry.*

"What if you were to go sit down next to Ben," I continued. "Tell him you're sorry and that you don't blame him for being mad at you. You could tell him that if he's not going to play, you're not going to play either. And then stay sitting next to him. Just sit with him in silence and wait for him to believe you. He might believe you. But Sam, he may not believe you within the hour; he may never go back in the game. So don't do this unless you are willing to give up the entire class period. You have my permission to just run over there, apologize quickly and then go right back in the game."

I then called loudly enough for the rest of the class to hear, "Sam run over and apologize to Ben, and you can get back in the game."

Sam decided that day to lose 30 minutes of playtime, rather than lose a friend.

Ben had a standard about friendship. A standard that said, "Friends don't do that to each other." Every kid in the gym heard me tell Sam he could get back in the game. Sam chose to keep himself out of the game. Five minutes before the end of the class period, Ben got up with Sam and they ran back into the game together. Both Sam and Ben finished the day with dignity and integrity.

Chapter Two

THE MIRACLE OF FORGIVENESS

I am no longer a school teacher. Today I am a marriage and family therapist. I collected a lot of stories as a teacher and I continue to collect a lot of stories as a marriage and family therapist. While the stories are different, the theme remains the same.

A number of years ago, a married couple came to me for counseling; I will call them Tom and Sue. They came in with a mixed bag of emotions about their situation. Tom had had an affair a few months earlier. He had fully confessed his wrongdoing and felt he had demonstrated an appropriate amount of remorse for his indiscretion. He believed that the tension that remained within their marriage was due to Sue's inability to forgive him for something that was over and done with.

Tom's thinking came from a strong desire to fix things. He asked, "What more can I do? I *said* I was sorry, and I really meant it. As a Christian, doesn't she have some responsibility to forgive and forget?"

Sue's thinking came from strong feelings of betrayal, a sense of inadequacy as a wife, and a sense of shame for not being able to truly forgive her husband. Sue said, "I want to forgive him, I just don't know if I can trust him anymore."

Tom wasn't sure how much longer he could wait for things to get better; "If she doesn't trust me, then maybe this whole thing just isn't going to work."

As a result, Sue felt even more pressure to hurry up and forgive. She didn't quite know what to do.

Sue had a standard about marriage. A standard that said, "Spouses don't do that to each other." She couldn't bring herself to accept less than her standard. To her it felt like "forgiveness" was requiring her to lower her standard. Self-respect and respect for her husband would somehow be compromised through this thing called forgiveness. Why? Because Sue was not convinced yet that she and Tom had the same standard. She didn't believe him.

To Sue it felt like Tom was not asking her to *forgive* his trespass — it felt like he was asking her to *overlook* it. If Tom wants forgiveness to happen *within* the marriage — he has some waiting to do. The waiting will not be about Sue finally choosing to forgive. It will be about allowing the time that is necessary for her to believe that Tom is truly sorry and hates his hurtful behaviors as much as she does.

Choice or Miracle?

We put a lot of pressure on each other as Christians to forgive. We expect forgiveness from a Christian (at least a good Christian). We're taught that forgiveness is a choice, and we are to choose to forgive. And so we try to muster up enough strength, enough willpower, to go to someone and say, "Oh all right! I forgive you." We may even try to sound earnest when we say it: "I want you to know that I forgive you." (It's the holy approach.) It can make us feel good about ourselves for a moment or two, until that determination to forgive subsides, and then we feel guilt and shame for failing when just a few weeks, or days, or even hours later we are faced with those same feelings of unforgiveness.

I explained to Tom and Sue that I didn't believe forgiveness was a "choice" — at least not for me. I cannot simply choose to forgive. I can't generate it within myself and make it happen. If it were a choice, we would all choose it and be done with it. Bitterness and resentment are exhausting.

Life has taught me that forgiveness is a miracle, not a choice. While I don't create miracles, I do experience miracles — even the miracle of forgiveness. Miracles lie beyond my natural ability; they require something supernatural. Forgiveness is something God supernaturally works in my heart by the power of truth.

> *Forgiveness is something God supernaturally works in my heart by the power of truth.*

Sue needed the truth; either the truth that Tom *was not* committed to the marriage, or the truth that Tom *was* committed. Healing and forgiveness would require the truth. And Sue wasn't quite sure yet what the truth was about Tom's commitment to her.

I told Tom that I understood how very hard it must be to wait for Sue's trust to return. "It's hard to wait; most people don't. So if you want to put a timetable on this you can; most people do. Let Sue and me know how much longer you are willing to wait, so that if she doesn't trust you or forgive you in that amount of time, you can both agree to get on with your lives. End the marriage, move on, and start over."

I asked Tom, "How much longer do you think you can wait? Three months? Six months? A year? A lifetime?"

Tom looked at me, then he looked at Sue, then he looked back at me, and back at Sue. Finally Tom said, "I will wait a lifetime if I have to."

And when he spoke those words, the miracle of healing began. Both Sue and I felt his sincerity. We believed him. His thinking had changed right before our eyes. He was ready to wait with Sue.

Living by a Standard

We may hear Sam and Ben's story and think — "Oh, that's child's play." We may hear Tom and Sue's story and think — "That's about adultery, something that will never happen to me." On the spectrum, in between child's play and adultery, are hundreds of hurtful indiscretions, hundreds of mindless moments of neglect, a lack of consideration, a lack of gratitude. We send countless messages, however subtle, that cause the people we love to feel like they have not measured up. To feel like they should have done things differently; they should have done things "my" way.

All of these unresolved hurts that accumulate over the years begin to make the relationship feel less safe — less inviting. It doesn't take long before there's less relating in the relationship. The reality is, just like Ben had a standard about friendship, and Sue had a standard about marriage, so do you and I have a standard about our relationships. Over the course of time, our standard will be challenged as being unreasonable, unimportant, ridiculous, or even petty. And our standard begins to change. It is lowered. Our relationships will only be as good as the standard we set for them.

> *Our relationships will only be as good as the standard we set for them.*

We all know what it is like to be in a waiting mode, where we are waiting for things to get better — for the trust to return. How is it possible for us to experience this process of healing? How can the miracle of forgiveness become our reality? How does forgiveness find its way into our lives and into our relationships without our standard being lowered?

Chapter Three

GOD WAITS

Scripture describes two different types, or standards, of love in the book of Luke. One of the standards I am very good at:

> 66 If you love those who love you, what credit is that to you? For even sinners love those who love them. And if you do good to those who do good to you, what credit is that to you? For even sinners do the same. And if you lend to those from whom you hope to receive, what credit is that to you? Even sinners lend to sinners, to receive as much again. 99 *Luke 6:32-34*

That standard I am capable of. It seems possible on a good day. Human nature is capable of that standard. It is natural for us to respond in kind: you give to me — I will give back. You be kind to me — I will be kind in return.

Jesus has a standard of love that is *not* natural; it is supernatural. He describes His standard to us in the sixth chapter of Luke:

> 66 But I say to you that hear, love your enemies, do good to those who hate you, bless those who curse you, pray for those who abuse you. To him who strikes you on the cheek, offer the other also; and from him who takes away your coat do not withhold even your shirt. Give to everyone who begs from you; and of him who takes away your goods do not ask them again. And as you wish that men would do to you, do so to them. 99 *Luke 6:27-31*

This standard, this kind of love, is not natural; it is supernatural.

How do we reconcile this supernatural kind of love with forgiveness? What thoughts go through your mind when you think of this standard of love and how it relates to forgiving someone? Does it cause you to consider the idea that maybe Sue does have some kind of responsibility to forgive and forget all of Tom's indiscretions? What is she waiting for? She should just be a good Christian and put it all behind her.

This supernatural love kind of looks like God just wants us to overlook sin, doesn't it? Are we supposed to ignore what we think and feel when other people cross one of our boundaries? Do we just "forgive" the hurtful sins of others? Is it our goal as Christians to "just get over it?" It's easy to get confused, isn't it?

How and when does forgiveness happen in the human heart?

Jesus Addresses Sin

We need to get clear on how Jesus addresses sin and on how He grants forgiveness. In one instance He will immediately say to the sinner, "Your sins are forgiven, go and sin no more." In another instance He will challenge the sinner harshly, as He did with the Pharisee when Jesus called him a "whitewashed tomb," or when He called some of the religious leaders "a brood of vipers." Jesus was so indignant at what was going on in His Father's temple that He went in, turned the tables upside down, and chased away the money changers.

How do we begin to understand the standard of love that Jesus puts before us? How does it impact the way in which we experience this thing called forgiveness?

Jesus did not march into the temple and say, "You have turned my Father's house into a den of thieves, but I forgive you, go and sin no more." No. And when He called the religious leaders a brood of vipers, implying that they were a danger to those around them and that their words were like poisonous venom, Jesus didn't say, "Oh well, I want you to know your sins are forgiven, go and sin no more." No.

God Waits to be Gracious

Like Ben and Sue, God too, waits for the miracle of forgiveness to happen. Isaiah 30:18 tells us "God waits to be gracious to you." He waits. He waits to forgive you your sins. But He is God... So what is He waiting for?!?

> "God waits to be gracious to you."
> Isaiah 30:18

I can understand why we might have to wait in order to experience forgiveness. When some injustice is done to me there is an immediate risk that some root of bitterness or resentment will spring up in my heart. There will be no forgiveness happening when bitterness or resentment is present.

On the flip side, when legitimate accusations or valid complaints about some wrongdoing come against me, it is likely that I will want to defend myself. Instead of seeing any error on my part, I might want to justify my position. There can be little forgiveness when my goal is to make myself "right." There will be no forgiveness when my goal is to shift the blame off of myself and put it onto another. But God has never succumbed to the sins that so quickly and easily spring up in our hearts. So then what is God waiting for?

If Tom or Sam had run to God and *quickly* asked for forgiveness, would they have *quickly* received forgiveness? Or would God have needed to wait just like Sue and Ben needed to wait?

I sensed that both Sue and Ben wanted to forgive (as does God), so what is the waiting all about?

Chapter Four

REPENTANCE vs. APOLOGY

The Bible is clear about what must precede forgiveness.

John the Baptist cried out, "Repent, and be baptized... for the forgiveness of your sins."[1] Repent and experience the grace of God.

Repentance

True repentance will include sorrow, a change of heart and mind, and a turning from sin toward God.

1) Repentance involves a change of mind.
2) Repentance involves a change of heart.
3) Repentance involves turning toward God.

Repentance is not just an outward show of regret. It is not just a simple verbal apology. Repentance requires something to happen internally, not externally. It involves a change of heart and mind. Repentance leads

> *Repentance requires something to happen internally, not externally.*

us to an all-encompassing recognition of wrongdoing. It causes us to see the truth about ourselves, and the truth about how our choices impact others. When we see *that* truth, we see what God sees; we are in agreement with God. When we see *that* truth, we see a need for forgiveness.

Looking for Signs of Repentance

The thing that Sue and Ben were waiting on was *repentance*. Rather than Tom being offended by the fact that Sue didn't trust him, Tom needed to realize that he had given Sue good reason not to trust him.

Sue was looking for signs of repentance:

- Was Tom truly sorry for what he did or was he, for the most part, just sorry he got caught?
- Did Tom hate his sin, or did he only hate the consequences of his sin (the consequence that his wife didn't trust him anymore)?
- Did Tom see a need to be forgiven?

Sue didn't want to simply "overlook" Tom's infidelity. To overlook something is NOT to forgive something. Sue wanted to know what was in Tom's heart and mind. And Ben... Ben wasn't looking for a "cheap" apology from his best friend. He wanted his friend to understand the hurtfulness of his behavior —

> *To overlook something is NOT to forgive something.*

the wrongness of it. Ben was more concerned about Sam's heart than Sam's behavior.

Cheap Apologies

We learn early in life the idea that a "cheap apology" is a noble thing. We might say to a young child, "You go over to little Susie right now, tell her you are sorry, and give her back that toy." Most of us are guilty of offering a cheap apology, and of asking our children to offer a cheap apology.

We would do better if we focused on our child's heart, not just his or her behavior. Instead of forcing an apology, we would do well to ask about what's going on in our child's heart, and to point out what's going on in the other child's heart... "Are you aware that when you took that toy away from Susie, it made her sad? Can you help me think of what we can do to make things right?"

The child can help come up with the idea of returning the toy and learning how to take turns. At the end of it all we can say, "I am proud of you for being so kind." Whereas, when we force an apology, it is often followed up with, "Don't you ever let me catch you doing that again."

Hmm... don't get caught. We teach our kids that getting caught is the problem.

Simple apologies are more about form than function. Apologies don't always serve us well because they don't always get to the heart of the problem. They don't reveal the condition of the heart, nor do they serve to turn the heart toward God.

Both Ben and Sue were looking for more than an outward apology. They wanted the truth about what was in the heart. Their waiting was both reasonable and responsible.

> *Forgiveness is not waiting on an apology, it is waiting on repentance.*

We want to learn to see life from God's perspective.

> 66 The Lord sees not as man sees; man looks on the outward appearance [which is why we offer simple apologies], but the Lord looks on the heart. 99 [2]

Forgiveness is not waiting on an apology, it is waiting on repentance.

Chapter Five

BLINDNESS TO SIN

I'm going to give you an abbreviated history lesson about a man named David.

David was a very wealthy king. Because he was a king, he was free to do whatever he pleased. That is one of the perks that goes along with being a king. David woke up one morning, took a stroll out on the palace rooftop, took a look over the edge, and there she was, Bathsheba, the wife of Uriah. One look led to another and Bathsheba soon found herself pregnant with King David's child.

Uriah was away from home, dutifully fighting in a battle for the king. When Bathsheba became pregnant, David wanted to cover up his mistake, so he conjured up a plan that allowed Uriah to leave battle and return home to "be with" his wife. But Uriah was too noble and faithful a warrior. He would not enjoy the comforts of home while his comrades were still at war. Ultimately, King David ordered Uriah to be put on the front line in battle where he was sure to be killed. The plan worked.

This piece of history does not portray David in a very good light. The beloved King David committed adultery, tried to cover up his mistake, and finally had Uriah put to death. But the most unsettling part of this whole situation is that for nearly a year David did not confess his sin because he did not see his sin. After all, David was king and kings are free to do what they please. David felt entitled to whichever women he wanted.

Problem or Sin?

David knew he had a problem as was evidenced by the fact that he tried to cover up his mistake. But his response does not indicate that he understood how deeply he had hurt and betrayed Bathsheba, Uriah, and his nation. David's reaction depicts a man who was dealing with a problem, not with sin. David was not owning his guilt, he was attempting to avoid being guilty.

Like David, we can attempt to control our problems by covering them up or pushing them aside. We think if we can control our problems by keeping them hidden, we can keep ourselves free from guilt. Sin, on the other hand, will require us to own our guilt.

God eventually sent the prophet, Nathan, to David after Bathsheba gave birth to his child. Nathan told David a story about a very rich man who stole a very poor man's only pet lamb.

> *Sin will require us to own our guilt.*

"Then David's anger was greatly kindled against the man; and he said to Nathan, 'As the Lord lives, the man who has done this deserves to die; and he shall restore the lamb fourfold, because he did this thing, and because he had no pity.'"[3]

Nathan looked directly at King David and told him, "You are the man."[4] David was at last able to see his sin. His eyes were opened to the truth.

Part of the miracle of forgiveness requires that we see our sin. Just like David, we need help in seeing our sin. Our human nature is constantly fighting to keep us free from guilt. Human nature is what we are born with — natural man, born in the flesh; that is how we refer to the condition of sin we are born into. In order for us to see the truth about ourselves we need to be able to see from a supernatural perspective, not a natural perspective. Like David, we need God to help us see our sin.

The Complacent Life

Those of us who have been Christians for a while may think we are safe from falling into the trap that David found himself in. Therefore, it is important when we hear King David's story to remember exactly who David was:

- David is referred to as the "man after God's own heart."[5]

- He is described as the "man who was raised on high, the anointed of the God of Jacob, the sweet psalmist of Israel."[6]

- David had loved and served God from his childhood.

- God had performed many great things through him and for him. (Remember Goliath?)

- David had praised God more gloriously than any other man.[7] (Read the Psalms.)

David was a very godly man who grew complacent in life. When life became easier for David he stopped looking to God for help and direction. As a result, we can see how quickly and how deeply David fell into sin. And worse yet, how long he remained unaware of his sin.

Surely if it was that easy for David, "the man after God's own heart," to overlook his sin that we would consider to be so large, then how easy would it be for you or me to overlook our sin that we would consider to be so small? The truth is, sin in any size is sin.

Sin breaks our relationship with God. "The soul that sins shall die."[8] Sin is not something to take lightly. We should all be very concerned about our blindness to sin. If only it were our hearts' desire to see our sin, then we could better guard our relationship with God and with others. In a world that tolerates and renames sin, we can boldly go to God in prayer... "Father, teach me to know my sin."

"I believe with all my heart that we will only experience the incredible grace of God in proportion to how clearly

> *We will only experience the incredible miracle of forgiveness in proportion to how clearly we see our need for it.*

we see our sin."[9] We will only experience the incredible miracle of forgiveness in proportion to how clearly we see our need for it.

Our loving God desires above all else to lead us to repentance so that we see a need for forgiveness. In being forgiven we stand ready to forgive, because in being forgiven we stand ready to love. In the next chapter we learn that, "He who is forgiven little, loves little."[10] And he who is forgiven much, loves much.

Chapter Six

FORGIVENESS FOR THE SINNER

In the seventh chapter of Luke, we are told about a Pharisee that invited Jesus to dinner. Jesus accepted his offer, and while Jesus was dining with the Pharisee we are told that a woman who was a sinner came and wept at the feet of Jesus...

> 66 One of the Pharisees asked him to eat with him, and he went into the Pharisee's house, and took his place at table. And behold, a woman of the city, who was a sinner, when she learned that he was sitting at table in the Pharisee's house, brought an alabaster flask of ointment, and standing behind him at his feet, weeping, she began to wet his feet with her tears, and wiped them with the hair of her head, and kissed his feet, and anointed them with the ointment. Now when the Pharisee who had invited him

saw it, he said to himself, 'If this man were a prophet, he would have known who and what sort of woman this is who is touching him, for she is a sinner.' And Jesus answering said to him, 'Simon, I have something to say to you.' And he answered, 'What is it, Teacher?' 'A certain creditor had two debtors; one owed five hundred denarii, and the other fifty. When they could not pay, he forgave them both. Now which of them will love him more?' Simon answered, 'The one, I suppose, to whom he forgave more.' And he said to him, 'You have judged rightly.' Then turning toward the woman he said to Simon, 'Do you see this woman? I entered your house, you gave me no water for my feet, but she has wet my feet with her tears and wiped them with her hair. You gave me no kiss, but from the time I came in she has not ceased to kiss my feet. You did not anoint my head with oil, but she has anointed my feet with ointment. Therefore I tell you, her sins, which are many, are forgiven, for she loved much; but he who is forgiven little, loves little.' And he said to her, 'Your sins are forgiven.'

Luke 7:36-48

He who is forgiven much, loves much. He who is forgiven little, loves little.

> *Forgiveness is for the sinner. It is only for the sinner.*

In looking at the Pharisee and at the woman, we see that the problem was not that there wasn't much to forgive in either of them; the problem was that one of them did not see his sin. The prostitute saw herself as a sinner; the Pharisee saw himself as being "pretty good." The Pharisee did not see a need to be forgiven. Here's the thing about forgiveness... forgiveness is for the sinner. It is only for the sinner.

> **"**Those who are well have no need of
> a physician, [only] those who are sick;
> I have not come to call the righteous,
> but sinners to repentance. **"**
> *Luke 5: 31-32*

Only the sinner will come to repentance. And only the repentant will find forgiveness.

Jesus said to the woman, "Your sins are forgiven."

The unconditional love of God did not overlook her sin. Jesus acknowledged her sin with her. They both agreed about her sinful condition. She knew the truth about her life and Jesus knew the truth about her life. Together they looked into her stained, hardened, sinful heart and Jesus offered her a new one. Jesus took the sin and threw it all into the depths of the sea.[11] He removed it as far as the east is from the west.[12] He made her entirely clean.[13] The unconditional love of Jesus caused her to have a complete change of heart and mind. She turned whole-heartedly toward the one who offered her a brand new beginning.

When Jesus removed the sin, He also removed its power over her. He removed the power of shame and its crippling effects. But one thing He did not remove; the knowledge of her sinfulness. The knowledge that she was a sinner. *That truth* God wanted her to keep.

That truth is what frees us from the bondage of ongoing sin. *That truth* is what causes us to hate the sin and desire to sin no more. Jesus was at last able to forgive her because she desired to turn toward God. She had had a change of heart and mind. She was repentant.

Seeing Our Guilt

In this account we see clearly what Jesus *does do* for the woman who was a sinner. He offers her forgiveness for all her sins, which were many. But let's also look at what Jesus *does not do* for the Pharisee. He does not offer him forgiveness. Neither of them verbally asked for forgiveness, and yet throughout scripture Jesus freely offers it to some and not others. Let's look more closely at who He offers forgiveness to and who He does not.

> 66 The Lord, the Lord, a God merciful and
> gracious, slow to anger, and abounding
> in steadfast love and faithfulness, keeping
> steadfast love for thousands, forgiving
> iniquity and transgression and sin, *but who
> will by no means clear the guilty.* 99
> Exodus 34:6b-7a (italics added)

Our merciful, gracious, loving, patient, faithful Lord
who forgives iniquity, transgression, and sin — will by
no means clear the guilty. The guilty are those who do
not see their guilt! The Pharisee, in his own mind, was
"not guilty." He saw the prostitute as being *bad* and he
saw himself as being *good*. His perceived goodness, his
self-righteous perspective, was the very thing he was
guilty of. Those who do not see their guilt see no need
for forgiveness.

Chapter Seven

AS WE FORGIVE OTHERS

66 Forgive us our trespasses *as we forgive those who trespass against us.* 99 [14]

God will forgive our sins as we forgive the sins of others. In other words, God is waiting on repentance, because only the repentant heart is truly ready to forgive. The unrepentant heart is not ready to forgive. The unrepentant are quick to judge and lack compassion. In the eighteenth chapter of Matthew we learn about how important it is that we are able to forgive:

66 The kingdom of heaven is like a king who wanted to settle accounts with his servants. As he began the settlement, a man who owed him ten thousand bags of gold was brought to him. Since he was not able to pay,

the master ordered that he and his wife
and his children and all that he had be
sold to repay the debt.

At this the servant fell on his knees before
him. 'Be patient with me,' he begged,
'and I will pay back everything.' The servant's
master took pity on him, canceled the
debt and let him go. 🙶🙷[15]

Here is a king who demonstrates his ability and
willingness to show compassion and mercy. When the
servant asks for time to pay his debt, the king offers
him more than time — he is willing to cancel the debt
completely. Let's read on and see if the king's mercy
brings about a change of heart and mind in the servant.

🙶🙷 But when that servant went out, he
found one of his fellow servants who owed
him a hundred silver coins. He grabbed him
and began to choke him. 'Pay back what you
owe me!' he demanded. His fellow servant
fell to his knees and begged him, 'Be patient
with me, and I will pay it back.' But he refused.
Instead, he went off and had the man thrown
into prison until he could pay the debt. When
the other servants saw what had happened,
they were outraged and went and told their
master everything that had happened. 🙶🙷[16]

Here is a man with an unrepentant heart. After being offered forgiveness for a tremendously large debt, he refuses to forgive a very small debt that is owed to him. This servant does not see the hypocrisy of his situation. He begs for mercy, but has none to give. He does not see his guilt, and the king who was willing to pardon him will by no means clear the guilty. Let's look at how the story ends.

> 66 Then the master called the servant in. 'You wicked servant,' he said, 'I canceled all that debt of yours because you begged me to. Shouldn't you have had mercy on your fellow servant just as I had on you?' In anger his master handed him over to the jailers to be tortured, until he should pay back all he owed. This is how my heavenly Father will treat each of you unless you forgive your brother or sister from your heart. 99 17

It would have been vastly better for the servant had he been able to see the truth that was in his heart. The king would forgive his servant as his servant forgave others. Being unable to forgive others, the servant was not forgiven.

Yikes! It is imperative that we are able to forgive others! What will make us able to forgive? The answer is, we must see the truth about ourselves. That is what will bring us to repentance. We must see our own need to be forgiven, and in seeing that need we will begin to have a change of heart and mind. Until that change comes about, we will not stand ready to forgive the sins of others. Yet, my blindness to sin may hinder me from seeing the truth. Therefore, I need help, I cannot rely on myself! There is too much at stake. Let's make this our prayer, "Heavenly Father, give me eyes to see and a heart to understand."

Apart from the miracle of repentance, we are left with nothing but our own feeble attempts at behaving in forgiving ways. Our willpower is not enough. It leaves us with a standard of love that will fall short. "If you lend to those from whom you hope to receive, what credit is that to you? Even sinners lend to sinners, to receive as much again."[18]

> *Until we see our own need to be forgiven we will not stand ready to forgive the sins of others.*

We must come to repentance.

Repentance is what will enable us to forgive. We must have a change of heart and mind. The servant in the story had no such change. He very quickly lost sight of his need for forgiveness. Had the servant in the story kept his focus on his own need to be forgiven, he would have been less focused on exacting payment from others.

The Prostitute and the Pharisee

In the previous chapter, the repentant prostitute who wept at the feet of Jesus was entirely focused on her own need for forgiveness. Because of that she did not focus on the sins of others, including the Pharisee. I believe she stood entirely "able" to forgive the Pharisee's sins, including the sin of his hurtful self-righteous condemnation of her.

If the Pharisee had wanted forgiveness, she would have been prepared to give it, for she understood that she too, stood in need of forgiveness. God had miraculously given her eyes to see and a heart to understand. Therefore, she would not have had to rely on her own limited ability to respond with mercy. She would not have had to muster up enough willpower to forgive him; she was entirely able. The Pharisee, on the other hand, did not see a need to be forgiven. He was not at all focused on his own sin, which made it very easy for him to focus on the sins of others. He was not prepared to forgive the sins of the prostitute.

The question we must ask ourselves is not, "Do we choose to forgive?" but "Are we able to forgive?"

The Blessing of Repentance

God waits for us to come to repentance because that is what will free us to forgive others. It's not that God won't accept our simple apologies as though He were unable to forgive; God is wanting and able to forgive. God waits because He knows that repentance is where we will find healing from life's hurts. That is when we will stop worrying about the sins of others.

We must see the truth about ourselves. "The truth will set you free."[19] The truth comes from the Spirit of

Truth — the Holy Spirit. As the Holy Spirit does His work in our hearts and minds, we begin to experience the fruit of the Spirit; the fruit of love, joy, peace, patience, kindness, goodness, faithfulness, gentleness, and self-control.[20] Through repentance we will experience the additional fruit of rest, humility, and freedom. God, therefore, waits for repentance. Isn't it good that God waits? Everything we long for in life hinges on our experiencing the fruit of repentance.

God needs to work a miracle in our hearts — the miracle of repentance. With repentance we will miraculously experience the forgiveness of our trespasses as we forgive those who trespass against us. Both blessings will become ours; the blessing of being forgiven, and the blessing of being able to forgive the sins of others. When we experience the miracle of forgiveness, we will see repentance not as a requirement, but as a blessing.

> *When we experience the miracle of forgiveness, we will see repentance not as a requirement, but as a blessing.*

The prostitute who wept at the feet of Jesus revealed a repentant heart and God responded to her heart. There is, indeed, more to forgiveness than the mere asking for it. God looks at our heart.

God Looks at Our Heart

As Jesus hung from a cross, there were two other men hanging with him; one on either side. The hearts of both men were revealed that day and Jesus responded, even on a cross, to a repentant heart.

> 66 One of the criminals who hung there hurled insults at him: 'Aren't you the Christ? Save yourself and us!' But the other criminal rebuked him. 'Don't you fear God,' he said, 'since you are under the same sentence? We are punished justly, for we are getting what our deeds deserve. But this man has done nothing wrong.' Then he said, 'Jesus, remember me when you come into your kingdom.' Jesus answered him, 'I tell you the truth, today you will be with me in paradise.' 99 *Luke 23:39-43 NIV*

One man hanging with Jesus saw the truth about himself, the other did not. When we don't see the truth about ourselves we cannot see the truth about Jesus, and we cannot receive from Him what He is prepared to give — forgiveness for our sins. The second criminal denied his need for a savior. Denial prevented him from seeing the truth and receiving God's gift.

Chapter Eight

OUR DESPERATE NEED

Outside of the truth, denial will begin to permeate how we see all of life. Denying our weaknesses hinders our ability to go to God in truth as we really are.

We are weak but He is strong...

As a young child I often sang a song that spoke truthfully about God's strength and my weakness.

> 66 Jesus loves me this I know,
> For the Bible tells me so
> Little ones to Him belong,
> They are weak but He is strong. 99

What an important reminder for us as we grow into adults. I am weak and my strength depends on my knowing my weakness. When I forget that simple truth, I might make the mistake of going to God with an imagined strength.

> 66 And they brought [a] boy to [Jesus];
> and when the spirit saw him immediately it
> convulsed the boy, and he fell on the ground
> and rolled about, foaming at the mouth. And
> Jesus asked his father, 'How long has he
> had this?' and he said, 'From childhood. And
> it has often cast him into the fire and into
> the water, to destroy him; but if you can do
> anything, have pity on us and help us.' And
> Jesus said, to him, 'If you can! All things are
> possible to him who believes.' Immediately
> the father of the child cried out and said,
> 'I believe; help my unbelief!' 99
> *Mark 9:20-24*

Here is a desperate father seeking help for his son. He asks Jesus, "*If you can* — help us."

And Jesus responds with, "*If I can!* All things are possible to him who believes." Jesus is challenging the man's faith. He is asking, "Do you believe?"

The father's response is one we can learn from. He says, "I believe; help my unbelief!" This father believes that Jesus is the one who can heal his son. But the father is saying more than this. He is saying, "I believe," but not enough to heal my son. If my son is healed it will be because of *your* belief, Jesus, not mine. "Help my unbelief!"

The father doesn't go to Jesus with any false ideas about his faith. The father isn't putting the life of his son in his own ability to believe or his own measure of faith. The father is fully aware that his faith is too weak. The father doesn't simply "choose" to believe.

He knows his choice to do so would be ineffective. It would fall short. Instead, he goes to Jesus in truth as he really is — with only enough faith to go to the one whose faith is enough. "Help my unbelief!"

The father knows that the miracle he is looking for is beyond his capability. Jesus helps the man's unbelief. Jesus takes the truthful measure of faith that the man has to give, and He adds His own measure of faith. The father's faith, when combined with Jesus' faith, is more than enough faith.

The father went to Jesus in truth with his limited faith. Where forgiveness is concerned, I believe Jesus also wants us to go to him in truth with our limited ability to forgive. My fear is that when we rely on our own ability to "choose to forgive," we are not seeing the truth about our limitations.

> *Our choosing to forgive might be the very thing that prolongs our inability to forgive.*

Our choosing to forgive might be the very thing that prolongs our inability to forgive. We are believing in ourselves. In essence, we are saying, "I forgive!" as though that were enough. And I fear it is not enough. When we give to God the truth that is in our hearts then we may follow our statement of forgiveness with, "Help my inability to forgive."

Help Me

Faith and forgiveness — two miraculous gifts that God works in our hearts. How small is our measure of both? If we had faith the size of a mustard seed we could say to a mountain, "Move." And it would move.[21] What that tells me is... I don't have enough faith to fill a mustard seed. It would not make sense for me to boast of my great faith. My hope is that God will continue to grant me enough faith to run to the one who has the measure of faith that I need. Jesus. My hope is that God would give me the clarity to run to the one who is able to forgive and say, "Help me forgive," rather than, "I choose to forgive."

Our greatest strength is to rely on the strength of our Father God. When we run to Him with our desperate need for help, He stands ready to receive us.

Chapter Nine

TURNING TOWARD THE FATHER

The Parable of the Prodigal Son[22] — a misnomer if ever there was one. We've all heard this parable in relation to the younger rebellious son. But this parable is not just about a younger son. The parable begins by telling us, "There was a man who had two sons...." This parable is about two sons, not just one. Here is the parable in a nutshell: There was a wealthy father who had two sons...

The Younger Son

The younger son was very rebellious and wanted nothing to do with his family. The young son asked his father for his share of the inheritance, indicating that he didn't really care if his dad was dead or alive. He wanted to take his inheritance, run off, and do with it whatever he pleased. The younger son was happy to take his father's money; the money he wanted, the father he did not. He had no sense of belonging to his father or family. He was content to disown all family ties.

The father, surprisingly, divided his money and gave the younger son his share of the inheritance. The younger son immediately left home and squandered his money on prostitutes and wild living. After he had spent everything, the younger son found himself in need. So much so that he ended up eating with the pigs because no one would give him anything.

The son finally had a change of heart and mind. He decided to turn toward his father; he decided to go home and say to his father, "Father, I have sinned against heaven and against you, I am no longer worthy to be called your son; please make me like one of your hired men."[23]

So the younger son went home. When his father saw him coming from a long way off (implying that the father must have been watching and waiting, hoping that his son might return), he ran to his son, threw his arms around him and kissed him. The son tried to apologize to his father, but the father (seemingly oblivious to the apology) quickly ordered the servants to bring the best robe, put a ring on his finger and sandals on his feet. Kill the fatted calf so we can have a feast and celebrate! Yay! That is the story of the younger son.

The younger son had a change of heart and mind, and turned toward his father. Forgiveness from the father was a moot point — the father had always been ready and waiting to forgive.

This parable then goes on to talk about, not just one lost son, but two lost sons. The other son, the older brother, was also lost. He was lost in his very own backyard.

The Older Son

Let's go back to the beginning of the parable and take a look at Jesus' audience. The first verse of chapter fifteen informs us that tax collectors and sinners were gathered around to hear Him (people that could perhaps relate more to the younger rebellious son). In the second verse we learn that Pharisees and teachers of the law were also there to hear Him (ahh — people that were perhaps more like the older son). Jesus is speaking to His entire audience. He is not just talking to the tax collectors and sinners. This parable is focused, I believe even more, on challenging the self-righteous, judgmental religiosity of the Pharisees.

Let's look at the older brother...

Out in the fields, where the older brother was hard at work, he heard music and dancing. So he asked one of the servants what was going on. "Your brother has come home," the servant said, "and your father is celebrating his return." The older brother became angry and refused to go in to the celebration. His father went out and pleaded with him to come in.

The older brother responded, "Look! All these years I've been slaving for you and never disobeyed your orders. Yet you never gave me even a young goat so I could celebrate with my friends. But when this son of yours [not this brother of mine] who has squandered your property with prostitutes comes home, you kill the fattened calf for him!"[24]

The father reminds the older son, "Everything I have is yours. Now we must celebrate and be glad, because this brother of yours [not this son of mine] was dead and is alive again; he was lost and now is found."[25] And that is where the parable ends. In essence, it ends without an ending. We are left not knowing whether the older brother decides to enter into the celebration or whether he decides to stay alone in the field. Does he go home with his father, or does he refuse his father's pleading to come home?

The Pharisees

In this parable, Jesus is not talking to the sinners around Him who already see their need for God's forgiveness. Rather, He is pleading with the Pharisees in the crowd to see how lost they are. He wants them to see that they are the older brother. Their obedience to the law does not put them in relationship with the Father. The Pharisees have a relationship with the law, not with the Father. They rely on the law in order to earn their goodness. They trust their goodness more than they trust God, and they love their ability to be good more than they love God.

> *Their obedience to the law does not put them in relationship with the Father.*

Their value comes in keeping the law. In fact it is their very obedience to the law that is keeping them from going home. It is keeping them from turning toward their Father.

This story targets not just "wayward sinners" who break all the rules; it also targets very religious people who do everything the Bible asks. Jesus is speaking to the Pharisees. In this parable Jesus points out that both those who throw away God and those who do everything God asks of them can be spiritually lost.

The self-righteous life of the Pharisee is actually portrayed in this parable as being the more dangerous life. The wayward younger brother was ultimately able to see his sin and eventually desired to turn toward his father and be with his father. The older brother in the story was never able to see his sin (because of his goodness), and continued to have no desire to be with his father. The older brother focused on his goodness and because of his goodness, he believed he was entitled to his father's things.

It turns out the older brother was no different than the younger brother. When the younger brother left home he felt entitled to his father's things. He did not love his father, he only wanted his father's things. The older brother did not love his father either. He only wanted his father's things. This parable is about two brothers representing two different ways to be alienated from God the Father, one through being "bad" and one through being "good."

Both "goodness" and "badness" can potentially corrupt our human nature. Both can prevent us from being in an honest relationship with God.

In his book *Prodigal God*, Timothy Keller writes:

> "The younger brother knew he was alienated from the father, but the elder brother did not. That's why elder-brother lostness is so dangerous. Elder brothers [the self-righteous] don't go to God and beg for healing from their condition. They see nothing wrong with their condition, and that can be fatal. If you know you are sick you may go to a doctor; if you don't know you're sick you don't — you'll just die."[26]

What role does forgiveness play in the lives of the father and his two sons? The father already has forgiveness in his heart for both his sons; he simply waits to give it. He waits and hopes for repentance to happen in their hearts and minds. He waits for his sons to turn toward home.

The father is entirely *able* to forgive. He simply longs for the *opportunity* to extend the forgiveness he already has in his heart, to his sons.

Ready to Forgive

The younger son was the first to have a change of heart and mind. The father demonstrates his eagerness to forgive. In having received his father's forgiveness, the younger son stood ready to offer forgiveness in his relationships with others. My guess is that when the rebellious younger son took his inheritance and left home, he may have had a critical, even loathsome attitude toward his legalistic judgmental older brother (who was probably pretty good at doling out shame).

Upon his return, I'm guessing the younger brother was not inside the house gloating over his newfound status as an accepted son. No, I'm guessing he was grieving like his father over the unresponsive heart of his older brother. I believe he now stood ready to forgive — even wanting to.

The parable ends as the father continues to wait on his older son. No doubt he will stand by the window and watch for his older son to come home just as he did his younger son.

> *Sin in whatever form it comes, breaks relationships.*

It was the sin of both sons that broke the relationship with their father. They both had a sinful mindset that caused them to feel entitled to their father's things. Whether it's a self-centered, rebellious mindset or a self-righteous, legalistic mindset, sin, in whatever form it comes, breaks relationships.

We need to see the brokenness.

If we don't see the brokenness, we will see no need for a change of heart.

Chapter Ten

BROKEN RELATIONSHIPS

The Lost Sons

When a relationship is broken, we need to make sure that the person we are in relationship with sees that it is broken. Without their seeing it, there is no hope for change.

The parable discussed in the previous chapter helps to make this point clear. In order for the younger son to see his sin, the father had to "let him go" his own way. As painful as it must have been to give his son all that money and then let him go off and squander it, the father didn't try to control his son. No doubt the father tried to *influence* his younger son, but in the end he didn't try to control him.

The father, again, could not control his older son. He had to let his older son return home or not. The father was left waiting and hoping for a change of heart and mind. I don't believe the father enjoyed having to distance himself from his two sons. I believe it broke the father's heart.

Tom and Sue

When Tom had an affair, it broke the relationship. It was up to Sue to make sure that Tom understood that the relationship was broken. If she did not make that clear, then nothing would change, including Tom's heart and mind. If there was no price tag to Tom having an affair, then Tom would more than likely have another affair. Sue's trust in Tom was broken. Healing for the relationship could only come if Tom had a change of heart and mind. Without Tom's repentance, Sue could not feel good about entering back into that marriage.

I don't believe Sue enjoyed having to distance herself from Tom for a while. I believe it broke her heart. And yet that is exactly what needed to happen in order to help Tom see the consequences of his behavior. Tom needed to see that he had broken the relationship. The brokenness was due to his sin, not her inability to forgive.

Tom wanted Sue's forgiveness. He found himself trying to manipulate that forgiveness. He tried to pressure Sue, even shame her into offering that forgiveness. "Doesn't she have some responsibility as a Christian to forgive and forget?" (Those were his very words.)

Something in Sue's spirit prevented her from extending that forgiveness. Tom felt entitled to Sue's forgiveness. Tom was unable to see the truth about his behavior. He was unable to be at fault; he was unable to be wrong. When we cannot look squarely at our wrongdoing we cannot be influenced by the truth. A sense of entitlement hinders repentance and forgiveness. Putting the blame and responsibility for the state of the marriage on Sue was like putting salt on a wound.

Sue truly wanted to forgive Tom. But to stay in the marriage without the necessary repentance would strip Sue of dignity and self-respect. Sue would not remain in a marriage unless both she and Tom held the same standard for that marriage.

The Spirit of God in her was telling her to wait. Stand ready — but wait. You see, Sue wanted the marriage to work, and she knew that their marriage would only be as good as the standard they shared for their marriage. She wanted the standard to be one that allowed them to look fearlessly into their own hearts.

Sue was looking for repentance in Tom's heart. A repentance that indicated he was dealing with sin and not just a problem. Sue stood ready — but she would by no means clear the guilty. The guilty are those who do not see their guilt. Sue did not see herself as being better than Tom. And she was not looking to punish Tom. She simply waited for him to see his sin and have a change of heart and mind. Sue's *ability* to forgive was not contingent on Tom being repentant. No. Her *opportunity* to extend forgiveness was contingent on Tom being repentant.

> *The guilty are those who do not see their guilt.*

Chapter Eleven

A CHANGE OF HEART

Our *ability* to forgive is not contingent on anyone else's heart. The ability to forgive rests on our heart alone. It would be cruel if our ability to forgive hinged on someone else's heart. A life of freedom and peace hinges on whether or not we stand ready to forgive.

When we are injured emotionally by another person, we sometimes believe the lie that we cannot be well until the person who wounded us sees how he or she has hurt us and seeks forgiveness. We develop a mindset that says, "You wounded me, you heal me."

> 66 We expect that healing can only come from the one who wounded us. We want them to see their wrongdoing and understand the ugly effects of their sinfulness. We get trapped into thinking that not until they feel remorse and beg for forgiveness can we become well. If a certain person or

> persons caused the problem, then it is only natural that we would go to them in hopes that they will fix it and make it right. That however, could be a long and futile wait for some of us. 99 [27]

The idea that our wholeness and wellness is contingent on the people and circumstances in our lives is a commonly held belief. Yet nothing could be further from the truth. Healing does not come when someone who has hurt us sees their need to be forgiven. Healing comes when we find ourselves able to forgive — whether they see a need for it or not. Just because a person asks for forgiveness does not make us able to forgive. If Sue were not *able* to forgive, it would not matter if Tom's heart came to repentance or not. She would be left unable to receive his repentant heart.

The Victim's Mindset

When the miracle of forgiveness is supernaturally brought about in our hearts, we cease to view ourselves as a victim. We begin to understand that we all have the same propensity to sin. We are all in a position to be the perpetrator and we all need God to protect us from holding that title. I have been hurt by

> *When the miracle of forgiveness is supernaturally brought about in our hearts, we cease to view ourselves as a victim.*

others, sometimes on purpose and sometimes without their even being aware. I, too, have hurt others — the worst part being that often I am unaware.

When we are self-absorbed in our own low self-esteem we grow unable to see outside of ourselves. God alone can give us eyes to see — ourselves first, and then the hearts of others. God alone can free us from the bondage of a self-focused preoccupation with avoiding further hurt from others. Victims tend to be on guard for whoever would wound them next. When we are focused on protecting ourselves from others, we cannot be mindful of loving others.

True freedom in Christ will give us a fearlessness that enables us to look into the hearts of others and respond in a way that makes room for the Spirit of God to work. Sometimes that God-like response will offer immediate forgiveness (when we see into an individual's heart and discern true repentance). And sometimes a God-like response will require us to respond in a way that leaves room for the Spirit of God to bring about conviction in the heart of the other.

Whether or not that conviction happens is between God and that person. We can open our own heart to God's truth, but we cannot force the heart of another. We can only wait for love to find a way. While Sue's response may have looked "unforgiving" to some, distancing herself from Tom was the most loving thing she could do. It made room for the Spirit of God to convict.

A glimpse into my heart

Many years ago while I was recovering from an abusive marriage, I desperately sought God in my need for solace. Had God pointed to the outrageous behaviors of my former husband my heart would have only been flooded with bitterness and resentment. If God had pointed to the guilt of my former husband, my human nature would have interpreted that as God implying my innocence. Therefore, instead of pointing to the sinful heart of the other, God pointed to my own heart. He helped me to see myself. He gave me a glimpse into my heart — a vision of my inner self.

In my mind's eye, I clearly and miraculously saw what looked like an ocean of seeds. God made clear to me that they were the seeds of every sin that I had the potential to commit. While many of those seeds lay dormant, most of those seeds were vibrating; they were waiting for an opportunity to spring to life. I realized it would be the grace of God that kept any of those seeds from growing. I got a glimpse of my enormous potential to sin. "For I know my transgressions, and my sin is ever before me.... Behold, I was brought forth in iniquity, and in sin did my mother conceive me."[28]

> Sin is conceived into me. I am made out of flesh and bone and sin. I saw what I was made out of, and I realized that sin is not something to be measured. 'The soul that sins

shall die.' (Ezekiel 18:4) We are not less guilty because our sins are less large. We are made out of sin. No longer did I stand wounded before God; I stood guilty before God. 🙵🙵[29]

The power of conviction is such that it does not invoke shame in order to destroy; it invokes guilt that leads to freedom. We are guilty; that's why we need a savior. It is not shaming — it is simply true. In seeing the truth about myself I developed a greater understanding of God's love for me. God sees the truth about me! And, God loves me. My perspective of myself changed from one of feeling inferior and inadequate, to one of being accepted and pursued in love by God in spite of myself.

Ironically, as God and I looked at my sinful nature together, it didn't cause me to hate myself, or question my value or lovability. On the contrary, it caused me to accept myself more. Because I saw clearly that God could not love me more. And it became possible for me to accept myself because I no longer had to try to accept a perspective of myself that was not true. I can believe the truth. It may not be pretty but it's true.

And God still loves me.

I no longer have to build a perspective of myself that struggles to find meaning or purpose or value. A perspective that requires me to prop up my identity with the idea that, "I'm not a bad person. I don't intentionally hurt people. I'm actually pretty good." I don't have to wrestle with those beliefs anymore because God has shown me:

- I don't need to believe in my goodness as though that is where my value lies. God says, "There is none that doeth good, no not one."[30] That includes you and me. God does not love me because I am good. He loves me knowing that His love will bring about in me a desire to be good. If any good comes from me it will be a blessing to me and to others. Not a measure of my value.

- I do not have to perform to a standard that makes me worthy or gives me value. My value is inherent. (It's a given.)

Nurtured by God's Love

Our life with God is not about trying hard to measure up. It is about being nurtured by His love so that we can live in the light and not in the darkness. We can live in freedom. The truth that we find in the light will set us free.

God loves you for free, simply because you are His. Nothing can separate you from His love. The amazing outcome of God's nurturing love is that it becomes possible for us to extend that same love toward others. The powerful, unconditional love of God becomes ours — ours to live in, and ours to give. We become free to love. That is how God blesses us. There is nothing more fulfilling than loving others well.

We must first see ourselves in truth as we really are. Psalm 51:6 tells us that God desires truth in our inward being. "Behold, thou desirest truth in the inward being; therefore teach me wisdom in my secret heart."

It is imperative that we see the truth about our sinful nature. When we see that truth, our prayer will become like David's, "Create in me a clean heart, O God, and put a new and right spirit within me."[31]

Chapter Twelve

THE TRUTH ABOUT OURSELVES

We are generally far more interested in others seeing the truth about *themselves*, than we are in seeing the truth about *ourselves*. Healing from life's hurts comes by way of seeing ourselves in truth. As truth pierces our heart we grow able to forgive. God brought healing to my own life not by magnifying the sin of the one who so deeply wounded me, but by magnifying my own sin. It seems so contrary to where our natural inclination would lead.

Too often we sabotage the work of the Holy Spirit by focusing on the sins of others. The Holy Spirit is hard at work trying to help us see our own propensity to do harm, while we are fighting to keep ourselves as blameless as possible. When we have a legitimate reason to be resentful, we *accept* our inability to forgive as being just that — acceptable. After all, we are only human, and pretty good ones at that. Such thinking allows us to minimize the idea that, "I too am a sinner."

When consoling others, we are sometimes quick to minimize the wrongdoing of the person we try to comfort. We are quick to agree that the fault lies elsewhere; perhaps we can point to a difficult childhood or neglectful parents. We may point to outside pressures that caused us to make bad choices. We help the blame to land elsewhere. And indeed blame will often fall on the other side. I am not trying to minimize the cruelties we sometimes endure in life. In fact there are times when our pain seems unendurable.

True consolation can look very different from what we might expect. I had the privilege of counseling a woman who came to see me after carrying around an enormous weight of sin for over twenty-five years. A choice she had made young in life left her with overwhelming feelings of shame. Through her tears she confessed what she had never before confessed — not even to the people closest to her.

Through my own tears I was able to, first, thank her for trusting her secret to me. And second, I was able to look at her and agree with her that what she had done was really awful.

She nodded her head in agreement, I nodded my head in agreement, and then we laughed. Yes, we laughed. Her relief was apparent. Her next words were, "Thank you for not making light of it."

I went on to tell her that however guilty she may think she is, in truth, she is far more guilty.

I then shared with her my story and the vision God had given me about my own sinful condition. She began to understand the unconditional nature of God's love, and the cleansing, redeeming power of His forgiveness.

As God reveals truth to us about ourselves, we become better prepared to stand with others in truth.

At the lowest time in my life when I desperately needed comfort, I experienced the very real presence of God. During that time God was able to both console me in my pain and require me to look more deeply into myself. He gently led me to the truth that was in my heart. How ironic that my healing did not come from being free of guilt, but of actually finding myself guilty; and how ironic that in understanding my guilt, I began to understand the enormity of God's love for me.

God's Perspective

The only place we will find an accurate and truthful perspective of ourselves is in God. His perspective of us is truthful. His perspective is not based on our performance; it is not based on our goodness, or our badness. Therefore, we are not at risk of losing

> *The only place we will find an accurate and truthful perspective of ourselves is in God.*

his love. He loved us while we were yet sinners. He loves us in spite of our propensity to sin. God's truthful perspective is that we, you and I, could not be more loved.

His love allows us to look at ourselves in truth and not fear what we see. His love provides a way for us to learn to hate the sin and desire to sin no more. He loves us enough to give us what we need to protect ourselves from the lies of this world. He gives us the Spirit of Truth, to teach us the truth.

When I see that God knows me and loves me, when I see that He offers me escape from the bondage of my sin, then I trust that His love is surely unwavering. He will not leave me or forsake me.

> 66 For I am sure that neither death,
> nor life, nor angels, nor principalities,
> nor things present, nor things to come,
> nor powers, nor height, nor depth,
> nor anything else in all creation, will be able
> to separate us from the love of God
> in Christ Jesus our Lord. 99
> *Romans 8:38-39*

The unconditional nature of God's love gives me solid footing when I need to pick myself up off the floor of despair. In dealing with the hurts of life, people are not the answer. God is. God knows what to do with sin. He will deal with the sins of others, and He will deal with my sin as well. It is enough for each one of us to work out our own life with God. Our only hope for finding forgiveness is to voluntarily walk into the light of truth.

Chapter Thirteen

LOVING THE LIGHT

Walking into the light of truth...

> **"** And this is the judgment, that the light
> has come into the world, and men loved
> darkness rather than light, because their
> deeds were evil. For every one who does
> evil hates the light, and does not come to
> the light lest his deeds should be exposed.
> But he who does what is true comes to the
> light, that it may be clearly seen that
> his deeds have been wrought in God. **"**
> *John 3:19*

"Whoever lives by the truth comes into the light."[32] It
may not look good (standing there in the light) — but it
will be true. According to Psalm 51:6, "God desires truth
in my inward being." God wants the truth.

We need to be able to look at a deed in truth (whichever side of the coin that deed falls on.) We need to be able to look at a job well done and say, "Yay! Look at what I did. It worked, and I love it." To do so is not boastful or arrogant. It's true! Whether it's a painting you've done, a project you've completed, or a room you've decorated. To minimize it would be a show of false humility or evidence of a lack of self-esteem. To delight in it would be to enjoy the creative abilities that God has blessed you with. When God got done creating stuff (the sky, water, animals, flowers), He said, "It is good!" And when He got done creating you He said, "It is very good." It's true.

We also need to be able to look at the other side of the coin, our failures, and say, "I blew it, I wish I had done that differently, I'm sorry, I was wrong." To do so is not weak; on the contrary, to do so is a sign of strength. It does not strip me of value, or diminish my worth. It is simply true.

When we don't have a truthful perspective of our lives, there is a good chance that we will participate in evil, that we will participate in something that destroys rather than heals. "And this is the judgment... men loved darkness rather than light, because their deeds were evil" (John 3:19). Our thoughts or actions may serve an evil purpose. Whether it causes me to hate myself or someone else, such evil will destroy.

If I attempt to keep my hurtful behaviors in the dark, I cannot see them or own them. I will only find the blessing of forgiveness as I stand in the light of truth.

Likewise, I cannot embrace the gifts and talents God blesses me with if I hide those gifts in the shadows, not wanting to draw attention to myself. The blessings of life will not be found in the darkness, but rather in the light.

"Wrought" in God

> 66 He who does what is true comes to the light, that it may be clearly seen that his deeds have been *wrought in God*. 99
> *John 3:19 (italics added)*

In order to avoid sin (whether by human ignorance or by design) my deeds must be wrought in God.

Wrought? I love those old words. I had to check the dictionary on this one: "Put together. Shaped by hammering with tools. Made delicately or elaborately."[33]

My deeds must be delicately hammered out and shaped by God.

I guess we've all got to be hammered on by God. Perhaps the reason John 3:19 closely follows the verse about how much God loves us "in that He gave his only Son," is because God's "loving us" will include His hammer.[34]

And isn't it interesting how God hammers on us? He doesn't hammer on us by taking control of our boundaries and making us do what He wants us to do.

He doesn't hammer on us with criticism or messages of disgust. He doesn't hammer us with messages of shame or rejection. No — He hammers us with the truth. He walks with us into the light (if we will go there with Him) and He reveals the part of us that we try so hard to keep in the darkness; the part of us that has the propensity to do evil — to do harm.

In the previous chapter, the woman who had kept her sin a secret for so many years, at last experienced freedom when she dared to bring her secret into the light. The Holy Spirit did not let up in His attempts to convict her of her sin and walk with her into the light. That is where she gave her burden to Jesus, and Jesus knew exactly what to do with her sin — it's gone. Her heart was repentant — He remembers her sin no more.

We will find blessing in the light of God's truth. As we experience the blessing, we learn to love light more than darkness. When we learn to love and trust living in the light of truth, we will be less vulnerable to being lured into the darkness.

Chapter Fourteen

DOORSTEP OF REPENTANCE

A long time ago, God asked Adam and Eve to not eat the fruit from a specific tree in the garden. They had every other food option available to them. Just not that one thing — the forbidden fruit. And sure enough, they both ate the "apple."

What did God do? He didn't scold them and put them to bed without supper. He didn't say, "No big deal, there are lots of other apples on the tree." He didn't say, "Oh well, go and sin no more." No. He kicked them out of the garden. He wanted them to know that they had broken their relationship with Him. It was swift; it was severe. There was no confusion.

They didn't go back to God and say, "Don't you have some responsibility, as God, to forgive and forget?"

God was clear.

I don't believe God enjoyed kicking Adam and Eve out of the garden. I believe it broke His heart. I believe it broke His heart that the consequence of their sin broke their relationship with Him. And not only did it break God's relationship with Adam and Eve, it broke God's relationship with every single person born of sinful man. We are all born into sin since the fall of man.

> 66 Behold, I was brought forth in iniquity,
> and in sin did my mother conceive me. 99
> *Psalm 51:5*

Sin is conceived into me. There is nothing I can do to rid myself of it. I cannot wish sin away. I cannot perform to a standard that would make me exempt from sin.

Sin was conceived into me. I am left unable to fix my condition of sin; therefore, I am left unable to fix my relationship with God. Why? Because God cannot co-exist with sin. If there is to remain a place free of sin, a holy place that is safe from evil, harm, and destruction, then God can have no part of me, for I am a sinner. God must protect heaven by keeping it free from sin.

Woe is me! I am in need of a savior!

I need to be saved from my sin. The son of God, Jesus Christ, has made a way for me to be saved. He has chosen to be my Savior. Only He could live the life that would allow me entrance into the holy presence and kingdom of God.

And He has chosen to live that sinless life on my behalf. He has lived it. And in dying He took upon Himself the death that I deserve. Because of that, He had to go to hell. That is the deserved punishment for my sin. He's been to hell and back again. Whether I appreciate it, or am even aware of it, He's already done it.

My part in it all is to accept the gift of salvation that His sinless life procured. With this gift I am reunited with God, a God who invites me to call him "Abba" — "Father."

Our Father in heaven has been waiting by the window watching for His children to return home.

In Relationship with God

We can return to a place of fellowship with our Creator Father who loves us with a love we cannot begin to understand. God longs to be in a relationship with us. He waits expectantly for us to have a change of heart, a change of mind, and turn toward Him. When Christ said on the cross, "It is finished," the curtain in Solomon's temple was immediately torn in two by God from top to bottom.[35] God was waiting. No longer must our sin separate us from God — our sin has been dealt with. On the other side of that curtain is where the Spirit of God dwelled. The Spirit of God now desires to have a new dwelling place. YOU! You can now be the very dwelling place of God. He wants to take up residency in your very soul.

We can be one with God. The only thing that prevents us from being in a relationship with God is our own inability to see our sin.

Please... see it, own it, and go to God in truth as you really are.

The people who see their sin are ready to receive the love of God. They are on the doorstep of repentance.

...To sinners Jesus would simply have to say, "Come down out of that tree Zacchaeus." And Zacchaeus jumped.[36]

...To the tax collector Jesus offered, "Follow me." The tax collector left his money on the table and followed Jesus.[37]

...To the adulteress who was thrown to the ground Jesus simply said, "Go and sin no more." Jesus knew he didn't have to give a sermon to convince her not to sin anymore.[38]

...To a small group of fishermen He said, "Come and I will make you fishers of men." They dropped their nets and followed Jesus.[39]

Jesus knows our hearts. He knows when all He has to do is hold out a hand and say, "Come." He knows when all He has to do is breathe on a group of men hiding behind locked doors and say, "Receive the Holy Spirit."[40]

Ask that the Holy Spirit of God be yours. Ask that He make His home in you. He waits for us to find ourselves on the doorstep of repentance. And He is right there, ready to forgive, ready to make His eternal Spirit one with ours. Repent, and receive from God the forgiveness of your sins and life everlasting.

Chapter Fifteen

STANDING READY

Sam and Ben

Sam deliberately went after Ben to get even. When he hit Ben smack in the face it wounded his best friend both physically and emotionally. Sam initially was blind to the hurt he inflicted.

I am still amazed at how quickly change can happen in the heart and mind of a child. I asked Sam a few questions, pointed to Ben's feelings, and it was over; I watched what was, for me, a five minute *miracle of repentance*. Sam owned his guilt.

As for Ben, I watched a thirty minute *miracle of forgiveness* as he got up with Sam and ran back into the game. I have not seen Ben or Sam for many years. My hope is that God continues to reveal truth to each of them in a way that rescues them from their goodness and their badness. My hope is that they remain as ready and able to see their own sin and to forgive the sins of others, as they were that day in the gymnasium.

King David

When King David finally saw the truth about his own sin, he realized that his life of privilege and social status was not a means by which he could get away with things that others might not get away with. His eyes were opened to his unhealthy sense of entitlement. He also realized that his past life of gloriously praising God and serving God was not enough to protect him from future vulnerability to sin. His good track record did not solidify his goodness. To rest in one's own goodness is a trap that will only cause blindness to our desperate need to rely on God's goodness. David's eyes were finally opened and he saw his true nature. He stood before God in truth. God's truth rescued him from his goodness and then from his badness. David stood before God in need of forgiveness. As David continued to be influenced by that truth, I believe he would stand ready to forgive.

The Bible is full of examples of people who needed the *miracle of repentance* to lead them to the *miracle of forgiveness.*

The Apostle Peter

The apostle Peter, one of Jesus' best friends, denied even knowing Jesus, not once, but three times the morning after Jesus had been taken captive. Just hours earlier Peter had promised to follow Jesus to prison and to death. Peter wept when he saw the truth about his own weakness and his inability to live the life he desired to live.[41] He didn't defend himself with all his good intentions. His years of following Jesus faithfully did not become his defense. Rather, it pointed all the more to his need for Jesus.

> *It is not about our faithfulness to Jesus — it is about His faithfulness to us.*

He realized, as we must, that in our relationship with Jesus, it is not about our faithfulness to Him — it is about His faithfulness to us. Through Peter's tears we see he had a heart of repentance. As a result Peter stood ready to forgive the sins of others. God's truth rescued him from his goodness and his badness.

The Apostle Paul

The Apostle Paul called himself the chief of sinners. He used to persecute and kill Christians.[42] When Paul saw the truth about himself and the truth about God's love, his ability to forgive others became a moot point. Paul would not be dedicating his life to worrying about and pointing out the sins of others. It was enough for him to work out his own standing with God. Paul stood ready to forgive the sins of others because he understood his own need for forgiveness. God rescued Paul from his goodness and his badness.

The prodigal son, the prostitute, the tax collector, the Pharisee, Tom, Sue, you, me... God rescues us all from our goodness and our badness. As we are rescued, our focus changes. Our hearts and minds turn. They turn toward God. We will find rest in God's unconditional love... and forgiveness toward others becomes a moot point.

Rescued From Our Goodness

We will stand prepared to forgive when we are so impacted by God's love that we understand:

- It is not about our faithfulness to Jesus, it is about His faithfulness to us.
- It is not about how good we are, how loving we are, or how gifted we are.
- It is not about how much we give, or how much we serve.
- It is not about what we have to offer Jesus, it is about what He offers us.

When we are impacted by that truth, then we are ready to be rescued from our goodness.

Rescued From Our Badness

We will stand prepared to forgive when we are so impacted by God's love that we understand:

- Despite all our wrongdoing;
- Despite all our self-seeking, self-serving, self-indulging, and selfish ambition;
- Despite our preoccupation with earning acceptance and approval;

- Despite the fact that we have looked to mankind more often than we have looked to God in order to find our worth and our value;

- Despite all of the hurts we have inflicted on others, knowingly or unknowingly;

- Despite anything that you may secretly add to this list;

Our heavenly Father stands ready to rescue us from our badness.

God loves us. He loves us with a love we cannot begin to understand. Go to Him right now, in truth as you really are. Ask Him to reveal truth to you. Ask Him to teach you how to love. Ask Him to forgive you, and ask Him to prepare your heart in such a way that you stand ready and able to forgive others.

God is with you and He will never leave you. When you find that you have wandered from Him, for whatever reason, you can be sure that He will be watching and waiting for you to have a change of heart, a change of mind, and turn toward Him. When we turn toward God we turn toward home.

Prayer

Father, help me to see my sin. Draw near to me as I walk into the light of truth with you. Teach me to love the light more than darkness. Give me eyes to see and a heart that understands my need for you. I come before you broken; needing your mercy and grace.

I give you my heart, my mind, my affections, my bitterness, my dashed hopes — all that I am, all I have become I lay before you. I am yours.

Oh Lord, may your love and grace flow through me and enable me to forgive others as you have forgiven me.

Amen

ACKNOWLEDGEMENTS

This is where I get to thank my big brother Bill for reading and editing this book, not just once, but many times. Thank you Bill! Your insights were invaluable. (You know which chapter is dedicated to you.)

Thank you Mary and Mom. Your edits were great.

Thank you Annie, for your suggestions and encouragement.

Crossroads Church is the church I call home. Thank you Crossroads for your support. Thank you for offering me a place to belong — a place where "No perfect people are allowed."

A huge thank you to Shellie. You make my work possible. I could not do it without you.

Thank you Lani. You are amazingly gifted at what you do.

Most of all, thank you family for being patient with me and eating out a lot while I wrote all of this. I love you.

ABOUT THE AUTHOR

Nancy Muyskens received her M.A. in counseling from Mid-America Nazarene University. She now practices in the Minneapolis/St. Paul area where she lives with her husband of 25 years. They enjoy living near their two children and son-in-law.

As an author and speaker, she combines her personal life, her counseling experience, and her faith in God to draw people into deeper and healthier relationships with God and with each other.

Discussion questions are available on Nancy's website.

www.nancymuyskens.com

PRAYERS and REFLECTIONS

_____

_____

_____

_____

_____

_____

_____

_____

_____

_____

_____

_____

_____

_____

_____

_____

_____

_____

NOTES

Chapter four
[1] Acts 2:38.
[2] I Samuel 16:7.

Chapter Five
[3] II Samuel 12:5-6.
[4] II Samuel 12:7.
[5] I Samuel 13:14.
[6] II Samuel 23:1.
[7] Nancy Stark Muyskens, *The Curtain is Torn* (Xulon Press, 2006), p. 18.
[8] Ezekiel 18:4.
[9] Nancy Stark Muyskens, *The Curtain is Torn* (Xulon Press, 2006), p. 18-19.
[10] Luke 7:47.

Chapter Six
[11] Micah 7:19.
[12] Psalm 103:12.
[13] John 13:12 King James Version (KJV).

Chapter Seven
[14] Traditional Matthean version of the Lord's Prayer found in Matthew 6:9-13. Note: These words are identical to the version found in the Litany section of the U. S. Book of Common Prayer, 1928 edition. (Italics added.)
[15] Matthew 18:23-35. NIV.
[16] Matthew 18:28-31. NIV.
[17] Matthew 18:32-35. NIV.
[18] Luke 6:34-35.
[19] John 8:32 NIV.
[20] Galatians 5:22.

Chapter Eight
[21] Mark 11:22-23.

Chapter Nine
[22] The Parable of the Prodigal Son, Luke 15:11-32.
[23] Luke 15:18b-19.
[24] Luke 15:29:30 NIV.
[25] Luke 15:31b-32.
[26] Timothy Keller, *Prodigal God* (Dutton, 2008), p. 66.
   I highly recommend his book and encourage you to
   read it in order to gain further insight into the parable.

Chapter Eleven
[27] Nancy Stark Muyskens, *The Curtain is Torn*
   (Xulon Press, 2006), p. 53.
[28] Psalm 51:3, 5.
[29] Nancy Stark Muyskens, *The Curtain is Torn*
   (Xulon Press, 2006), p. 12.
[30] Romans 3:12.
[31] Psalm 51:10.

Chapter Thirteen
[32] John 3:19, NIV.
[33] *The American Heritage Dictionary* of the
   English Language. New College Edition.
   Houghton Mifflin Company, 1976, p. 1478.
[34] John 3:16, John 3:19-21.

Chapter Fourteen
[35] Matthew 27:51.
[36] Luke 19:1-6.
[37] Matthew 9:9-11, Mark 2:13-14.
[38] John 8:10-11.
[39] Matthew 4:18-20.
[40] John 20:19-23.

Chapter Fifteen
[41] The account of Peter's denial is found
   in Luke 22:54-62.
[42] Paul claiming to be Chief of sinners;
   refer to I Timothy 1:12-17.

CPSIA information can be obtained at www.ICGtesting.com
Printed in the USA
LVOW080943280512

283558LV00001B/1/P